PRAISE FOR BETSY L. JORDAN

"I hired Betsy for executive coaching, and it was one of the best decisions I've made in a while. She revitalized key aspects of my career with her thoughtful and disciplined methodology. She is so intelligent and empathetic, yet she'll tell you when your full of sh*t when you need to hear it. I highly recommend her to turbo-charge your life."

—Chip Venters

CEO at BrowsePlay Interactive Video

"Betsy, brings a great energy and enthusiasm to her work. Creative, concise and fun to work with."

—Joseph C. D'Alessandro

Independent Media Production Professional

"Betsy is an inspired leader with energy and passion to share her many gifts and talents. I recommend her without reservation."

—Denise Cline
Member at Law Offices of Denise Smith Cline, PLLC

"Betsy exemplifies the word *transformation* for that is what she offers all of her clients. Coaching with Betsy offers direct feedback and direct results!"

—Laura Gould
Owner/Coach at SwimLessonsRaleigh.com

"North Carolina's film industry was well served through Betsy's insight, hard work and commitment. Betsy championed projects that promoted the industry and was able to focus on the key issues that made a difference in how North Carolina competed against other states. She's a great ally to have on your team."

—Monty Hagler
President & CEO, RLF Communications

"Betsy Jordan is a visionary who can see beyond the routine tasks of the day. She has a gift for marketing and putting together resources to accomplish her goals. Betsy is a leader and can influence others with her keen insight, clear communication style and engaging personality."

—Bob Jamieson

Living Seaside Realty Group

"Betsy is bright and highly intuitive. Her assistance with me at a critical point in my life's journey was instrumental in helping me in many areas, both professional and personal. Anyone hiring her will be rewarded many times over."

—Joe Christian

Performance Coach

"Betsy is an amazing business woman with dead-on intuition and a plethora of skills and experiences to draw from. I recommend her without reservation."

—Trish Thomas

CEO at Atomic20

"Betsy Jordan has a keen insight into helping people achieve their life goals. She has an uncanny knack for breaking down barriers that may be creating obstacles for people that they cannot see for themselves: a frequent life-staller; spending time with Betsy is like drinking from a cold fountain on an incredibly hot day; you always want to come back for more! Take making a change in your life seriously and give Betsy a call; you won't be sorry!"

—Anna Watson Blair
Infusion Therapy Nurse at UNC-Hospitals

"Betsy is a seasoned professional who brings her high energy level and professionalism to everything she does. Having her work with you and your company is a great investment."

—Teena Anderson
Non-Profit Organization Management Professional

"Betsy is a results oriented person, one you will be glad to have had the pleasure to meet, and delighted she's always working in your best interests."

—Carol Spiller, CMB

CONNECT!

BOOKS BY BETSY L. JORDAN

Seven Absolute Keys to Create Anything:
Stop searching for yourself and create your life!

BOOKS BY BETSY L. JORDAN

BullsEye!
The Seven Tactics To Hit The Bull's Eye In Your Business
Film Industry Professional's Edition

Book One: Connect!

Book Two: See!

Book Three: Act!

Book Four: Experience!

Book Five: Expand!

Book Six: Power Up!

Book Seven: Launch!

BullsEye! The Seven Tactics To Hit The Bull's Eye In Your Business

CONNECT!

The Seven Tactics To Hit The Bull's-Eye In Your Business

Film Industry Professional Edition, Book One

by Betsy L. Jordan

Editing, Cover and Book Design by Rodney Miles

Dedicated to the remarkable film industry professionals who contributed, using these tactics.

CONTENTS

PREFACE TO THE FIRST EDITION

Tactic One: CONNECT!

WELCOME TO *BULLSEYE!*, *The Seven Tactics to Hit the Bullseye in Your Business, Film Industry Professional's Edition!* I created this book series for simple reasons: I see too many of my friends in the film industry often uprooted (and then miss them!) and I see too many creative, talented, worthy people ride the ups and downs of available projects in a seemingly capricious industry, and it doesn't have to be that way!

In fact, in my career as a coach and consultant my team and I have seen how with your own simple *commitment* to changing your life and career for the better—for more income, stability, and happiness—and how with a simple *commitment* to adopting the hard-won principles and using the exercises in this series of books, your life can be changed forever. Please use them, please enjoy them!

This particular volume, *CONNECT!*, covers one of the most basic yet most powerful tactics we will, any of us, ever exercise, often with miraculous results. The amazing thing is that so many of us have all of these *connections* just lying around which we never fully realize, utilize, or nurture, yet it can be argued that life is only at its fullest when we do truly connect.

Philosophers and plowmen have understood this through the ages, and it's with great excitement that I encourage *you*, through these pages, to discover your own connections and foster new and improved ones, and watch your life and career blossom like a flower right before your eyes. It's exactly what I did with my film, *PowerTrack,* and the following text contains exactly how I did it.

We have divided this series into a total of *eight* books for several carefully considered reasons. Each of the seven tactics is individually addressed in detail in its own book, followed by a comprehensive volume titled *BullsEye!* which contains all of them. This creates a convenience and a focus as each tactic on its own offers opportunity for careful thought and specific exercises, or conversely, also makes available a compendium of all tactics and exercises in one volume for those perhaps more eager to sail through at a quicker pace or through repetition. So there will be some repetition from volume to volume, enabling each to completely stand on its own, but the heart of each will be unique to that tactic. We all have our own learning styles, and we hope that making these available as we have in different formats will open the doors to anyone to experience and enjoy, regardless of personal preference.

It's exciting to connect with you, and I hope we can meet each other also through any of my available opportunities at the back of this book, whether it's through personal BullsEyeCoaching™ or seminar and webinar opportunities.

Thank you for purchasing, reading, and most of all *using* this book and all it has to offer. I'm glad we've met.

—Betsy Jordan
Wilmington, North Carolina
September 2015

PART ONE:
UNDERSTANDING

INTRODUCTION ... YOUR BULLSEYE

The greater danger for most of us lies not in setting our aim too high and falling short; but in setting our aim too low, and achieving our mark.

—Michelangelo

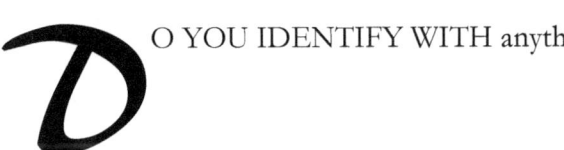O YOU IDENTIFY WITH anything like this?

- "I don't want to uproot my life, my family to chase another film."
- "I don't have a business degree so I don't know where to begin."
- "I know I'm talented yet don't know how to level things out to showcase my talents."

In the first book, *The Seven Absolute Keys to Create Anything!*, we discussed the principles "behind the curtain" so to speak. Now with the *BullsEye!* book series, we put the rubber to the yellow brick road.

This version—the film industry professionals' edition—is intended to provide anyone who wants to start a business venture in film with a specific set of tactics, to reveal what is working and what may be missing. This valuable system covers everything that the film professional needs, including specific exercises for "target practice."

Why are we sharing this with film professionals? Over the past twenty years we've observed firsthand the ups, downs, and sideways of the motion picture industry. I mean, I've produced, acted, and written screenplays myself so I understand the basics.

Creativity is just connecting things. When you ask creative people how they did something, they feel a little guilty because they didn't really do it, they just saw something. It seemed obvious to them after a while. That's because they were able to connect experiences they've had and synthesize new things.

—Steve Jobs

And we've noticed that everyone *waits* for the next movie, the next picture. Meanwhile, we do whatever it takes to survive. Years then go by and there's not a lot to show for it. *And I, personally, am tired and saddened when I see my film industry professional friends move away to chase that next opportunity when they could remain in one place were they to utilize the tactics in this series of books.*

Many of you try to start businesses only to have them shelved as you go to the next picture. It's heartbreaking to see so much talent especially when it's not channeled into something sustainable. My team and I have experienced the same thing.

Yet it doesn't have to be that way for you. Learning the seven tactics is the first step. The BullsEyeCoaching™ process (which includes the seven tactics)

Humankind has not woven the web of life. We are but one thread within it. Whatever we do to the web, we do to ourselves. All things are bound together. All things connect.
—Chief Seattle

is the best way to determine what your primary venture should be. With a little help, *you* can determine how to start and keep your business going. And in the process you learn how to troubleshoot when things aren't moving as quickly as you'd like. The BullsEyeCoaching™ system can be accessed by attending our seminars, and by going to our website and signing up for coaching.

Buy the book. Come to a seminar. Take the webinar. Hire a coach. Walk away with the venture designed specifically for you to hit *your* bull's-eye.

Chemistry is one of these crazy things you can't teach or learn or you can't fake. You go in hoping it will work, hope that you will connect with the other actors. I was fortunate on 'Modern Family' and 'The Procession.' They are great people, very easy to like.

—Jesse Tyler Ferguson

A NOTE TO THE FILM INDUSTRY

You are capable of more than you know. Choose a goal that seems right for you and strive to be the best, however hard the path. Aim high. Behave honorably. Prepare to be alone at times, and to endure failure. Persist! The world needs all you can give.

—*E. O. Wilson*

*H*I, AND WELCOME TO *CONNECT!* Book One in *BullsEye! The Seven Tactics To Hit The Bull's-Eye In Your Business.* This is the film industry professionals' edition.

My friends have been waiting and wanting to understand how their state government is going to support film *or not support film.* What if you didn't have to worry about that? What if you could take your unique skill set and your unique talents, integrate them with a few other principles and create your own sustainable and viable business based on your passion projects?

It's important to think good, speak good, and do good. If we want to see positive change in the world, then we need to connect to goodness. I try in everything I do, both in business and philanthropy, to make a positive change and do that by doing good.

—Shari Arison

This book series has the goal of your understanding a few key business concepts with an emphasis on understanding what to do, how to do it, and further how to tell what is working and what is missing. In fact you'll hear us talking about that a lot—getting you to ask, "What is working and what is missing?"

It's important to know the distinction between what you would like to do, and what you are best at. It's so easy to take these things for granted. Every film industry professional we know has some specific skill, or many times, several specific skills and talents and they could offer those skills and talents in a way to create value for a lot more people in the world than in just one motion picture.

And none of this should be a surprise. After all, you've been in the trenches! Some of you have been doing this for *years and years and years* and you find you've developed relationships across the country or across the world. Many of you are just getting started and you're trying to find your way and what was once a thriving market has changed a great deal given the political climate. The best thing that you can do right now is to discover your particular skill set and create it as a value proposition for a sustainable long-term business.

This is not to say that you stop doing motion pictures and you start working for other people, In fact I mean to encourage that you do both. Too often you get involved in a picture and then give it your all twenty-four/seven, and after it's done you don't have anything else to show for it.

The more aware of your intentions and your experiences you become, the more you will be able to connect the two, and the more you will be able to create the experiences of your life consciously. This is the development of mastery. It is the creation of authentic power.
—Gary Zukav

This series of books offers you system that will change that.

Unlike other self-help, human development, or business books that seek to emulate and observe other businesses to give advice, I speak from first-hand experience as someone who has gone down that road and lived to tell about it.

In fact I've worked in the lumber industry, in hospital supply products, in banking, in real estate, and in coaching. In fact a little about me might make this all more relevant. I'm from a small town. When younger I was a head lifeguard and a first-class Girl Scout. I attended University of North Carolina and earned a bachelor's of science degree in business administration, while active in student government and with the finance committee. From there I went on to hospital supply

Think about what people are doing on Facebook today. They're keeping up with their friends and family, but they're also building an image and identity for themselves, which in a sense is their brand. They're connecting with the audience that they want to connect to. It's almost a disadvantage if you're not on it now.

—Mark Zuckerberg

sales, then customer relations with First Union bank (remember them?). I was the director of marketing for a program to redevelop the inner city in downtown Raleigh.

I worked for my father's gubernatorial campaign. In fact, my sixteen years of advising public officials was in an "officially appointed capacity." It is clear that politicians get lots of advice from industry professionals, yet there were just twenty or so of us who were officially putting together policy.

After moving to Hawaii I sold boat trips and began my own meeting and event planning business. *Then, in 1992, I began acting and getting more involved in film.*

I produced and co-produced films such as *The Coldest Night in Georgia, The Last Summer,*

A great attitude does much more than turn on the lights in our worlds; it seems to magically connect us to all sorts of serendipitous opportunities that were somehow absent before the change.
—Earl Nightingale

PowerTrack, Sugarfoot, and others. And after getting married and having a beautiful daughter, began my own marketing company. In 1999 I went into coaching others. I have since grown my coaching practice and run for public office.

These days, while states across the country are bidding for film business, it causes much uncertainty for anyone to build a stable environment for themselves or their families in the film industry. After more than sixteen years advising pubic officials on ways to attract the film industry and incent the import of film projects, I decided to run for office, particularly to challenge obstacles to a long-term film agenda in North Carolina.

So while making a living doing what you love may seem in a lot of ways uncertain, isn't it exciting to

The world is being re-shaped by the convergence of social, mobile, cloud, big data, community and other powerful forces. The combination of these technologies unlocks an incredible opportunity to connect everything together in a new way and is dramatically transforming the way we live and work.

—Marc Benioff

think of, to imagine creating your business so that you can support your family and continue to do work you feel passionate about?

There are a definite, few *tactics* you can use to create *anything* in the world. The process begins when you have an idea. You then take the idea through a series of steps before it becomes a real-world thing, and as an example of my own, *PowerTrack* became a video. I'm going to quickly run through this process we undertook with *PowerTrack* because it's so valuable, and I want you to get an overview of how this works.

In producing a stock car racing video for kids called *PowerTrack,* which won several international film festival awards, throughout the video we showed people how to build a race car and showed how it was different from your family car, but the *PowerTrack* formula is one that you can use in many different business scenarios.

(1) SEVEN TACTICS

Strategy is buying a bottle of fine wine when you take a lady out for dinner. Tactics is getting her to drink it.

—*Frank Muir*

EACH OF THE SEVEN tactics (each covered fully in its own text, one of which you now hold) have a corresponding area of the body. You can easily understand and remember these tactics and their corresponding body areas just as child is taught songs that involve his and her head, shoulders, knees and toes and so on:

1. Our first tactic, Connect!, is associated with the crown of the head.
2. The second tactic, See!, is at the third eye or forehead.
3. The third tactic, Act!, is at the larynx or voice box.
4. The fourth tactic, Experience!, at the heart.
5. The fifth tactic, Expand!, is located at the solar plexus

or the diaphragm.

6. The sixth tactic, Power Up!, is located at the abdomen

7. And finally, the seventh tactic, Launch!, is located at the groin or the base of the spine.

Put them all together and you *hit your bull's-eye.*

~

The making of the film, *PowerTrack,* will be used as a working example throughout this book series, and *PowerTrack* began with the thought and the thought was about filming a video and selling it like one I'd seen done that apparently netted the creator a million dollars. They produced videos for two-year-olds and toddlers about big dump trucks, bulldozers, and big machinery

Walking is magic. Can't recommend it highly enough. I read that Plato and Aristotle did much of their brilliant thinking together while ambulating. The movement, the meditation, the health of the blood pumping, and the rhythm of footsteps... this is a primal way to connect with one's deeper self.

—Paula Cole

moving dirt. Two-year-olds would watch it forever and ever. This guy made over million dollars by taking out an ad in *Parade* magazine. When I read about this, I was between projects and considering what I was going to do next, and my team and I decided, "Let's make our own video!"

It's interesting when you try to emulate somebody else's idea, because it doesn't turn out exactly the same way.

I was talking to my stepsons at the time and I asked them, "What would you like to watch if you were making a video?" They said either sports or fast cars. Well, North Carolina is the home of NASCAR, so what better way and what better place to film anything having to do with stock car racing?

I think that connection with humans is so important. Sometimes I'll do this monologue and talk to the crowd, like, 'Come on, let's really connect here.' I don't think a lot of people understand it's a two-way exchange. Some people go to a show and are like, 'Yeah, you make me feel.' That's not how it works.

—Chet Faker

Connect

So after the *thought* happened, I then started thinking, "What are my connections?" And this was really the first step in getting going.

My father had run for office and through that experience I met many different people across the state. In fact I met a gentleman who worked at the head of NASCAR. He suggested I connect with someone at the Richard Petty driving experience. I visited my friend Dusty Powers, who is a videographer I know, and he connected me with David Baxter and Jim Tringas. I was following along with the connections I had or could make and the leads that I had at the time. So I went to talk to Dusty about editing *and he had just decided to open up his own editing studio.* This was a wonderful break

People are so fearful about opening themselves up. All you want to do is to be able to connect with other people. When you connect with other people, you connect with something in yourself. It makes you feel happy. And yet it's so scary - it makes people feel vulnerable and unsafe.

—Toni Collette

for us because it meant we had more control over the editing of the film.

See

The next is *seeing* beyond what others had seen before. So we took a look around and I really wanted to do what they call the *comparison game*—you know, "How long does it take a kid to tie his shoes?" compared to "How long does it take to change the tires, gas up the car and do everything you need to do in the pit." The comparisons didn't end there—we were *seeing beyond* where we were looking and saying, "Okay, how fast does a race car go? As fast as a rocket," and the comparisons continued.

con·nect
/kə'nekt/
verb
bring together or into contact so that a real or notional link is established.

Act

Then we decided we needed to take *action,* and this is not just me (or you, in your case) taking action, either. I started making phone calls followed by going to sit down in front of the folks at the Richard Petty Driving Experience, at the NASCAR headquarters in Concord, North Carolina.

Experience

I was *willing to experience,* and that made a difference. While picking up the phone and calling tons of people might be where some would stop, actually going in person and sitting down and meeting with people made all the difference. It was an exciting process. Every moment was a different experience than the moment before.

Talking with my friends and family every day helps keep me grounded and connected to home. They are the most important things to me.

—Colbie Caillat

Expand

We had *expansive* plans. We had decided we were going to include as many ideas as possible. We included Dusty and his editors, we included David and Jim, and we included the race car driver Jeff in all of our plans and designs. We really wanted to go right down there and film the stock car racing. I planned or hoped to include my stepsons Taylor and Kyle in the filming, too, and while Kyle was away at camp, Taylor was able to be in the film.

I am saddened by how people treat one another and how we are so shut off from one another and how we judge one another, when the truth is, we are all one connected thing. We are all from the same exact molecules.
—Ellen DeGeneres

Power Up

While looking to sell the film, of course, we also saw *PowerTrack* as a way of educating kids and it being a children's video product. We looked to NASCAR because we were told it was to be a racing

One's own self-worth is tied to the worth of the community to which one belongs, which is intimately connected to humanity in general. What happens in Darfur becomes an assault on my own community, and on me as an individual. That's what the human family is all about.

—*Wole Soyinka*

video, so I called a couple of production companies that were sanctioned by NASCAR and offered to split the profits with them 50-50 if they simply included *PowerTrack* in their catalogue. That was not what they wanted to do, so we continued to reach out and we submitted the video to international film festivals. We won two awards: the gold in Charleston and the silver in Houston international film festivals. We continued to reach out and finally were able to solidify a distribution deal with public libraries.

Launch

Once the video was produced and edited it was time to get the cover designed, to get the ISBN number, to get the video packaging designed, and to get everything ready to sell. And all of this was done with *ease*. I used my connections, I asked questions, I didn't mind going places, I was seeing the video completed, and thus it was.

Your Seven Tactics

Take the example of *PowerTrack* and you'll see that I ran it through all of the seven tactics, starting with the tactic of connection. This process when used for *your* business will look different, but it will in fact be the same. I find that the more you use the seven tactics the more second nature they become and the easier it is to integrate them as a process into your business so that you can level out your income, so that you can provide value to people that

You can't fake this music. You might be a great singer or a great musician but, in the need, that's got nothing to do with it. It's how you connect to the songs and to the history behind them.

—Etta James

are willing to pay for it, and so that you can support your family in the end.

So you see, when you start with *connect,* this system will help you design your business or venture the same way the *PowerTrack* project was designed. The difference will be that you get to integrate it from *you.* You get to integrate *your* business from *your* skill set, from *your* talent, and from *your* passion project. I was open and active to and with my *connections,* old and new.

A very dear friend is one of my best networking connections as well. Her name is Debra, and she created a public relations company for the architectural and interior design vertical, so she is very specialized in her focus. When she started this business the overall market took a dive and it became

We cannot live only for ourselves. A thousand fibers connect us with our fellow men.

——Herman Melville

difficult as people slowed their hiring of PR people.

But Debra, being Debra, was not daunted in the least. She used this time to go out and network. She went to everything she could. She talked to everyone she could. And in that time Debra developed more than *eighty* very solid connections directly dealing with her industry she had chosen to serve. Debra created solid business connections in that down time and these people have led her to other people. She is working now in both New York and in Boston, happily pursuing her passion projects within her specific skill set.

The beginning of a friendship, the fact that two people out of the thousands around them can meet and connect and become friends, seems like a kind of magic to me. But maintaining a friendship requires work. I don't mean that as a bad thing. Good art requires work as well.

—Charles de Lint

(2) ALL CONNECTED

I believe that two people are connected at the heart, and it doesn't matter what you do, or who you are or where you live; there are no boundaries or barriers if two people are destined to be together.

—Julia Roberts

*H*AVE YOU EVER WALKED into a room and felt someone's presence before you actually "saw" them there? Have you ever been thinking about someone who has not been in contact with you for a while, and then had the phone ring and it was them? Have you ever walked by a radio and caused it to become static, and what made you think it was *you* causing that? Maybe you walked away and the music played clearly again?

There is no secret here; if you are like most, you sense and seem to know we are all connected. My question to you is this: How can you use this knowledge in your business (and in your life), for more success and fulfillment?

First of all, choosing to believe that we are made up of the same stuff and recognizing that we are all connected you can then hit your bull's-eye. Will your business or venture be manifested rapidly through seeing this connection and living it? Yes, absolutely. Your experience of connecting with life on all levels, can surprise you with all sorts of support coming from unexpected places.

Use this tactic, then—allowing yourself to be consciously *connected*, to strengthen connections to people who work with you, your clients and your vendors. See where those connections are weak and notice your judgments. The judgments of others honestly, do not matter.

I was taken by the power that savoring a simple cup of coffee can have to connect people and create community.

—Howard Schultz

(3) TEFLON

Gratitude unlocks the fullness of life. It turns what we have into
enough, and more. It turns denial into acceptance, chaos to order,
confusion to clarity. It can turn a meal into a feast, a house into a home,
a stranger into a friend.
—Melody Beattie

ALL OF CREATION IS made up of the same stuff: nitrogen, hydrogen, and oxygen. And in the biggest picture—the biggest picture our minds can see, "it" all looks alike. The difference, as we will see, is in how we perceive "it," how we interpret "it," how we react to "it," and how we combine "it," where "it" is what we are creating in our lives, consciously or not. So Tactic One is CONNECT!.

Most of you would agree that you are already powerful, that you already create your own world. We are each unique examples of that same source incarnate (or in physical form). Some use the word "source," some use "Allah," "Yahweh," "Jehovah," or some use "energy." We believe it's all the same.

My family and I cook at home almost every day together. The kitchen is the central and most important room in the house; it's a great way for us to connect.

We love going to the farmer's market on Sundays is a family and choosing the ingredients together.

—Jose Andres Puerta

So for the sake of being on the same page and speaking the same language, let's suspend our religious or secular judgments. You are in that image, or likeness of God, or you are made up of the same "stuff" as everything else. My point is that you are already building your world whether you want to or not.

We're going to recommend you "put on the Teflon," which doesn't mean to disconnect, it really means to let go of taking things to heart or of automatically being defensive. Imagine that you could go a whole day, week, or month and never judge. We *naturally* assess our surroundings and the people around us. For example, sometimes in my not-so-distant past I judged my mother. She often gave me unwanted advice (How many of you have moms like this?). It's the stuff of major TV shows. And being a mom myself, I can assure you, TV portrays us accurately sometimes as nagging busybodies in our children's lives, but this is just my humble opinion.

Our judgments separate us. As we put on our Teflon and look at our businesses without defensiveness, we get ideas from unexpected places.

My former husband and I went through hours and hours of court battles. If we had both just stepped back and said, "My vision for my life is different from your vision;" if we had both been willing to "be okay" with our different points of view, the courts would not have factored into anything.

But an innovation, to grow organically from within, has to be based on an intact tradition, so our idea is to bring together musicians who represent all these traditions, in workshops, festivals, and concerts, to see how we can connect with each other in music.

—Yo-Yo Ma

Where there is judgment, there is a lack of trust. Acceptance is the only path to true connection.

~

Creativity is the power to connect the seemingly unconnected.
—William Plomer

So how does this apply to the hitting your bull's-eye? To connect with new and different clients and customers requires relating to them in accepting ways, even if you might not like everything that your clients want. We are all connected. When we "have on our Teflon," when we don't defend or take things personally, we can recognize connections more quickly and can create what sometimes appear to be *miracles*.

(4) CREATING YOUR BUSINESS

Men tend to be hierarchical, but women are driven to make lateral
connections so they can cooperate.

—*Helen Fisher*

L ET'S TALK ABOUT WORK relationships. The greatest partnerships or business relationships are created by two wholly independent people who choose to be together because they can and want to be together. Partnerships created based on dependency look like one partner being stronger than the other. These partnerships end up spiraling downwards for they are formed in the energy of contraction, of lacking and of fear.

When we talk about connecting we're talking about my favorite part of developing a business. It's about networking and being out in the world. So when you get invited to something or you decide that you're going to sit at home one day and not go to something that somebody invited you to, understand that you may have passed up an opportunity to connect. This is not to suggest you kill yourself trying to meet other people, but simply that when you're open to them, you will make connections that are unexpected, that will be useful, and that you can be useful too.

Many business manuals talk about connection in terms of networking, public relations, outreach, and so on. What we intend to do with the first tactic, connect, is to have you look at all of your connections. So when you've discovered what venture you are undertaking, and you have your plan for starting your business, you then look at all of your connections.

Starting a business is a commitment. You are committing to servicing your clients and to

I don't believe that life is linear. I think of it as circles - concentric circles that connect.
—Michelle Williams

being a creator of value. It is something that will take your time and effort. In this book series we are giving you a practical system you can use which will speed up your success. As you set your sights and aim for your targets, keep in mind that you are connecting for the purpose of giving your talents to the world.

Is it hard work? Yes. Does it have to feel that way? No. When you're making these connections with people—with friends, family, and with your community, ask for other connections.

Take a minute right now and open up a new document on your computer or take out a new piece of paper, and write down every sphere of influence that you have. Consider your connections with your:

If you look at history, innovation doesn't come just from giving people incentives; it comes from creating environments where their ideas can connect.

—*Steven Johnson*

1. family,

2. friends, and your

3. community, whether it's church, community involvement, or different groups.

I'm so thankful for the Internet because actors and singers and performers now have a way to connect with their fans on a very personal level which I think is quite special.
—*Ariana Grande*

List every name you can possibly think of. Put down your friends of friends, your friends of your family, the people in your life that are in your community, physicians, people who are in your industry, and any other outside areas of influence where you know people that you can talk to.

Take the time to schedule talking with these people and every day spend 30 minutes just connecting. In this way you will open up to new avenues and open up to new ways to take your venture or business public. Enjoy the process!

Just like when I was putting

together the *PowerTrack* video (and I keep using this because it's a great example of how my connections led to other connections), I spoke to everybody I knew about *PowerTrack*. I would share with them what I was doing and invariably, because people want to help people, I would have a new connection with every established connection I contacted. Keep a record of all these old and new connections, whether you write them down or organize them into contact management software.

In the film industry, unlike any other industry I have ever worked in, people tend to understand the metaphysical. This is the nature of things. We are all made up of the same stuff. The difference is how it's organized. What you want to call that quality that connects us, that power behind the organization

I work really hard at trying to see the big picture and not getting stuck in ego. I believe we're all put on this planet for a purpose, and we all have a different purpose... When you connect with that love and that compassion, that's when everything unfolds.

—Ellen DeGeneres

I don't know the first real thing about the dating game. I don't know how to talk to a specific person and connect. I just think you have to go to person by person and do the best you can with people in general.

—Jason Schwartzman

of it all—be it "God," "source," "nature," or whatever—makes no difference to me. What we want you to do is to know how to best utilize your power to connect for the good of your family, your friends, and your livelihood.

We've heard many people talk about the loss of the industry tax credits and incentives. And truly, it's important to create indigenous film everywhere. Everyone has a story to tell and everyone has a special gift that they can turn into value which will be rewarded.

I went to an actor's studio once with Orlando Jones who is becoming one of my personal heroes. Orlando has been in numerous films and television series from which you would recognize him. And Orlando says everyone has a story to tell and that is true. We all have stories to tell. Some of us tell their stories better than others.

Some of us write our stories. Some of us shoot (film) those stories. Some of us tell those stories. But all of us have a story to tell and all of us have a unique way that we tell our stories. So what we're talking about here in the first tactic of connecting includes connecting to your idea of your story to tell. Is your story about how you shoot a camera better than anyone else? Is your story about how you actually can put together details and produce things better than anyone else? Or is your story about how you can produce and manage people? And truly it doesn't matter if you are doing these things better than anyone else, it matters only that you're willing to say that you do this specific thing and that you figure

Jazz music is America's past and its potential, summed up and sanctified and accessible to anybody who learns to listen to, feel, and understand it. The music can connect us to our earlier selves and to our better selves-to-come. It can remind us of where we fit on the time line of human achievement, an ultimate value of art.

—Wynton Marsalis

By 'flat' I did not mean that the world is getting equal. I said that more people in more places can now compete, connect and collaborate with equal power and equal tools than ever before. That's why an Indian in Bangalore can take care of the office work of American doctors or read the X-rays of German hospitals.

—Thomas Friedman

out how to use the seven tactics to hit your bull's-eye and start your business.

We are seeking to create a business that will last through other projects. Even if you're called away on a film, the idea is to maintain your 30 minutes every day (or at least every week) and continue to make more connections. If you schedule the time and do this you will see results and be prepared with valuable connections when the time comes to work on your own project, business, or new venture.

Often people start a business because they think, "Okay I can do this. I have been doing this. I have the experience to do this. I have a skill set and a resume for this and obviously people will pay me to do this at the level of my expertise." Do not however underestimate the value of *connection*. While it is true that who you know gets you in the door, your talents and skills will keep you in the door, but only as long as you maintain your connection with people. So the next time you think about burning a bridge, understand that the person you're dealing with right in front of you may be connected to at least a thousand other people. These connections matter.

Stay with me now for powerful exercises to get you started!

As we get past our superficial material wants and instant gratification we connect to a deeper part of ourselves, as well as to others, and the universe.

—Judith Wright

PART TWO: COMPANION JOURNAL & EXERCISES

WHEN YOU PLAY A sport like tennis, there's often (hopefully) an occasion when the ball meets the racquet *just right*. We call it the "sweet spot." The following exercise will help you find the "sweet spot" in your connections with people, and leave you free to make the best choices.

It's time to embrace *commitment*. Commit right now to truly connect. These exercises actually take precious little time but often yield tremendous rewards. The time involved is a small investment but has often proven to be exceedingly worthwhile. You can spare the time, and after all, we never truly *find* time, we *make* it.

With each step of every exercise, space has been provided if you care to make notes on your experiences for future reference or interest.

Enjoy!

EXERCISE: MUSIC

Music is a moral law. It gives soul to the universe, wings to the mind, flight to the imagination, and charm and gaiety to life and to everything.

—Plato

1. Play music. Instrumental music works best. Simply close your eyes, whether standing or sitting, and allow your mind and body to follow the path of the notes.

2. Now move with the music.

3. Then stop the music. Sit or stand in silence. Notice the silence. Out of that silence, the music you just heard was born.

4. Make notes about this experience and about how you can use this silence, personally.

5. Discuss this with one or two of your friends.

6. Get them to experience the same thing in the car, or in a department store, or on an elevator. Have them listen to the music.

EXERCISE: BREATHING

Until I feared I would lose it, I never loved to read. One does not love breathing.

—*Harper Lee*

1. Find a comfortable chair.

2. Set an alarm or your kitchen timer for twenty minutes.

3. Turn off all the lights, silence all sound, and sit with your feet on the floor, hands comfortably in your lap.

4. Take three deep breaths and focus only on your breathing.

5. Continue to focus on your breathing. When your mind wanders—and it will—bring your attention gently back to your breathing. Continue this until the timer or alarm goes off

6. Make notes about this experience.

7. Focus on your feelings of connection, or judgment, depending on your experience. Note that judgment separates you from yourself and ultimately, from others.

EXERCISE: COMPARING

Comparing and contrasting is a valuable human skill - and not just during high school English exams. Our ability to rank-order things is invaluable in making choices and setting priorities.
—*Martha Beck*

1. In silence, walk outside in nature, feeling the ground beneath your feet. Understand that this ground is also moving and made up of the same thing as you are. It is simply moving so slowly that you cannot see it with your eyes.

2. Stop in front of something that you would like to observe more closely, such as a blade of grass, a flower, or a tree. (Do not choose another human being or a building.)

3. Sit or stand in front of this object and ask yourself the following questions:

a. How is this like me?

b. From where did this particular creation come?

c. How is this creation different from me?

d. How has this object changed during the time I
    have been observing it?

4. Now go to a public place or find a person.

5. In silence, gently look at people around you or at each other and notice what you see.

6. Think about how you would describe this person. What feelings are coming up? Does this person remind you of anyone? What are your feelings about that? How does it feel to look at someone so closely?

7. Now, for the interesting part, imagine that this person is really just one other possibility of *you*. Notice how you are similar, notice how you are different, and what is your judgment of this person now? What if you had zero judgments of this person?

8. Make notes on your experience.

9. Share with your employees and business associates how you might use the tactic of Teflon to create what you want in your business.

EXERCISE: YOUR INNER VOICE

Your inner voice is the voice of divinity. To hear it, we need to be in solitude, even in crowded places.

—*A. R. Rahman*

TAKE A FEW MINUTES and write down:

1. The ways you judge yourself. There is an inner voice which will say all kinds of mean things to you about you. Sometimes we are not aware of this, so tell someone to give you a compliment and see how you respond internally. That inner voice is usually your biggest critic.

2. The ways you judge others.

3.   Take each judgment and reframe it, turn it around.

EXERCISE: TRANSFORMATION

Life is a moving, breathing thing. We have to be willing to
constantly evolve. Perfection is constant transformation.

—Nia Peeples

*T*ACTIC ONE, CONNECT, EXPLAINS that if we are argue with someone nearby, the incident leaves a mark on someone else in another place. It's not a chain reaction or anything as clearly direct, yet it has this effect, just the same. It explains why Mother Teresa would say, "You will not see me at an anti-war rally. If you have a peace rally, please invite me." She understood connecting along with the other tactics. She knew we are all connected. She knew to focus on the thing that is highest and best to get the results that she wanted and she also knew that what she placed her attention on would expand. She took action.

All of the seven tactics overlap. The process is integrated and happens regardless of what we think about it. We are always breathing, our blood is always pumping. We create new cells in our body every second. With every thought that we think; we are creating. At the level of thought and emotion, we can affect things in the world that we do not see. We always have the opportunity to connect to launch, and to take action.

In the following exercise, when we tested it, we found that it was effective in demonstrating that we can affect others simply by our thoughts and feelings. I was surprised when we discovered that the person with their eyes closed would often respond or react and not even be aware of their reactions! I see this exercise now as a way to illustrate all of the tactics on a subtle level. It clearly shows that we affect others by our thoughts and that once we accept that we do, we can affect everything around us by never even saying a word.

1. Choose a facilitator.

2. Put one person in the front of the room with their eyes closed (possibly blindfolded).

3. The facilitator then whispers to each of the other participants a word such as joy, sexiness, frustration, and so on.

4. The participants go up one by one and without saying a word, they do their best to *generate* the word that they are given in the person who has their eyes closed!

When we did this, we were amazed at the accuracy of the silent transference of emotion. Try it in your business meetings, if you can do so with a measure of seriousness.

EXERCISE: CONNECTING & YOUR CROWN

You have brains in your head.

You have feet in your shoes.

You can steer yourself

in any direction you choose.

You're on your own,

and you know what you know.

And you are the guy

who'll decide where to go.

—Dr. Seuss

ACH OF THE SEVEN volumes of *BullsEye! The Seven Tactics to Hit the Bull's-Eye in Your Business* comes with a final powerful, specialized exercise for that particular tactic. And I know you will think this next exercise is silly. It is. But it's one of the most powerful, too. That I'm asking you to put your hand on top of your head, on your forehead and throat and so forth is silly. It is so silly in fact that you will remember it. And that's the point.

What if there were one exercise that could make you so

clear about the seven tactics that every time you do a creative project, every time you work on a business, every time you develop any new venture, you knew exactly what you were doing? What if you could always see what is working and what is missing so you can tweak what you're doing so as to hit your bull's-eye?

You can!

So here we go. Put your hand on top of your head and understand we are talking about connecting.

Many of us believe we are all only separated by 6-degrees but I want you to realize it's really a separation of *zero degrees,* as we are all connected. Many of us have the same experience of thinking about somebody and the phone ringing, it being whom we just thought of. We are all connected at the very base of it all. It doesn't matter what your religious beliefs are, we are all connected. You've likely heard before that we are all "one," and this is not just some metaphysical mumbo-jumbo. But we will talk in more practical terms. Whenever you decide on the talent that you're going to market, or what business venture you're going to start, or which film you're getting ready to produce as your passion project, it's going to be important that you can connect with people with other skill sets and with different audiences. [see Figure 1 and 2, next page.]

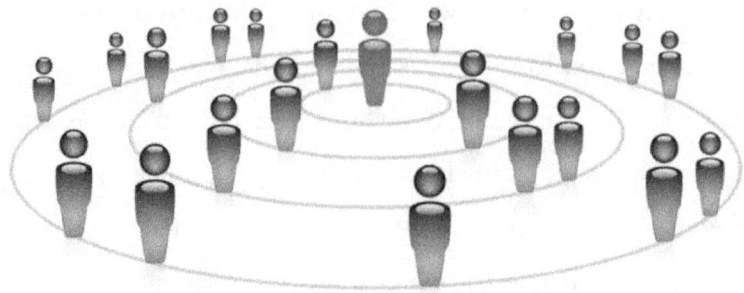

[Figure 1] "Six degrees of separation" is *actually* more like *one* degree.

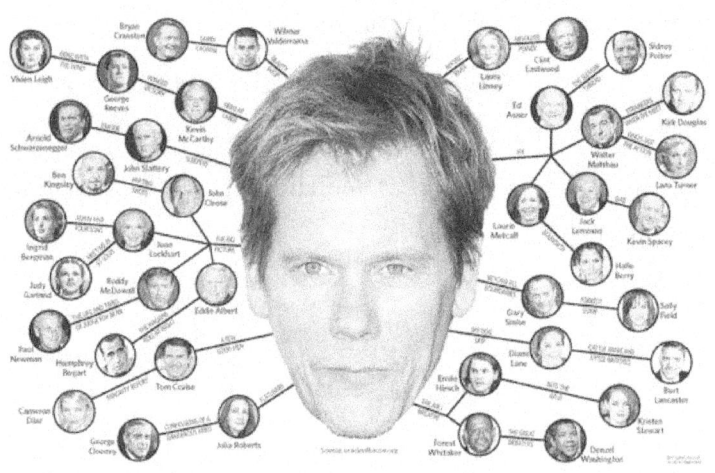

[Figure 2] It's even been shown that we are all connected with Kevin Bacon if we examine our own "connections' connections."

Talk about and consider these things as you simultaneously touch the top of your head. Realize connecting is associated with this part of your body.

EXERCISE: CONNECT!

A good idea will keep you awake during the morning, but a great idea will keep you awake during the night.

—*Marilyn vos Savant*

I F YOU HAVE A business or venture idea, take the time *right now* to *write* down five connections on the following pages. Call or email these people (calling is better). Talk to them about your new venture and ask for their help. Ask them for five more names, numbers, and email addresses. Keep notes about your conversations and do this daily:

1.

2.

3.

4.

5.

CONCLUSION

Imperfection is beauty, madness is genius and it's better to be absolutely ridiculous than absolutely boring.

—Marilyn Monroe

IT'S MY HOPE TO help you learn and make second nature the use of the seven tactics in your own life and in your business, so that no matter what role you play in the film industry you can create a business right where you are that satisfies your passion as well as your family's needs and wants in life.

If you decide to speed your assimilation of the seven tactics, you need to be willing to commit and do the work, to show up in a safe space for two days and attend one of our seminars. And those of you who want fast, powerful, individual and effective results, we offer one-on-one coaching. (For either of these services there is typically a waiting list. Please contact us to discuss the next available opportunity.)

Don't wait for some legislative body to make up their mind. Start today or continue to put one foot in front of the other. Develop your very own *bull's-eye*. By the time politicians have decided, you will be well on your way to stabilizing your business, you will have hit two or three of your own bull's-eyes.

We are, each of us, whole and complete beings. Using these principles does *not* mean that you lack in any way, but only wish to improve.

You *are* the one opportunity on planet Earth to be exactly who you are, at any given moment. "Fixing" someone or "making up" for their "shortcomings" is not the same as recognizing that someone is magnificent and holding them to a higher standard. May you celebrate your magnificence by embarking on your most miraculous project yet—yourself, and bring your special gifts to the world..

START TODAY!

THE TIME TO BEGIN your perfecting of the seven tactics is *right now*. Your full life of passion, your independence from waiting on politicians to gain their senses or the film industry to seek you out is at hand.

Buy and read the next volume in *BullsEye! The Seven Tactics to Hit the Bull's-Eye in Your Business,* by visiting this web page:

www.BullsEyeCoach.com

SEMINARS & WEBINARS

IND OUT ABOUT UPCOMING seminars and webinars by visiting this website:

www.BullsEyeCoach.com

COACHING

AND FOR YOUR QUICKEST route to perfecting the seven tactics and to experience The BullsEyeCoaching™ process (which includes the seven tactics), *contact me today.* I look forward to meeting you and hearing your ideas!

info@BullsEyeCoach.com

ACKNOWLEDGEMENTS

*T*HIS IS A WORK about life. I could say that I thank everyone who ever touched my life directly and indirectly for all of you have been teachers, and I mean that sincerely. In this way, you all have contributed to the writing of this book.

But there are people who influenced this book directly. First, thank you to my mother, who taught me to question why things are the way that they are. Second, my father, who taught me not to take all of this so seriously anyway—either I was going to do what I thought was best and get to heaven or, there is no heaven so still, do my best. It's a philosophy that has served me well.

To the town of Mt. Gilead. For those of you who have never visited, it did take a village to raise me and I believe every citizen in that town had a hand in my raisin'! To my friends in Hawaii who opened my eyes to the beauty of love in paradise, Joni, Michael, Jim, Richard, and Greg. To my brother who wears his heart on his sleeve yet still plays a mean hand of poker and handles his enormous responsibilities with intelligence beyond the pale. To my sister who thought I could do no wrong 'til she got wiser and realized that she's smarter than me, anyway. Thanks also to my brother in law, Carter who showed me firsthand the value of having a dream and doing it over again. And my sister in law, Wendy who showed me that fairy tales do come true.

To my friends in Charlotte who honored me as a leader in that city; you know who you are. To my friends in Raleigh/Cary who have been with me through the fire. To my talented and savvy Executive Administrator, Colleen, who knows more about me than she ever wanted to yet is so very graceful in her acceptance and fierce in her defense of our mission. For Robbie whose optimism and adroit communication brightened our way. To my mentors, all of you: Ray, Michael, Lori, Rob, James, Sam.

To my former husbands both of whom taught me the extraordinary strength and power of faith. To the great loves of my life who are numerous and so I would rather they know who they are and be grateful that we had that love. Once I choose to love someone, I *always* do, even if we disagree.

Sean Roach, I wouldn't have ever thought about <<writing these books>> if not for your brilliance and direction. And Rodney Miles, thank you so much for your contribution above expectations and execution of this series. I look forward to many, many years with this team of amazing people.

To the boys of my heart, Kyle and Taylor, who taught me that parenting had nothing to do with being of the same genetic make-up. And finally, to my sensitive and brilliant daughter who shows me every day what a miracle life is.

www.ingramcontent.com/pod-product-compliance
Lightning Source LLC
Chambersburg PA
CBHW051922170526
45168CB00001B/495